INVOLVING FAMILIES

in

Middle Level Education

John Myers
and
Luetta Monson

NATIONAL MIDDLE SCHOOL ASSOCIATION

National Middle School Association

When *Involving Parents in Middle Level Education* was published in 1985 the topic was in its relative infancy. Because of the recent expansion and interest in family involvement in education, Dr. Myers agreed to revise the 1985 publication. What follows is really a new publication. The Association is grateful to Dr. Myers and his colleague, Dr. Monson, for undertaking the task that led to this valuable publication.

Dr. John Myers is Associate Professor and Chairman of the Department of Middle Grades and Reading at West Georgia College in Carrollton. A former middle level teacher, he has served our Association as a member of the Publications Committee and currently is a member of the Editorial Review Board for *Research in Middle Level Education*.

Dr. Luetta Monson is Assistant Professor in the Department of Middle Grades and Reading, West Georgia College. Also a former middle level teacher, she is an active member of National Middle School Association and the Georgia Middle School Association.

Copyright © 1992 by National Middle School Association
4807 Evanswood Dr., Columbus, Ohio 43229-6292
Second printing, April 1993

The materials presented herein are the expressions of the author and do not necessarily represent the policies of NMSA.

NMSA is a registered trademark of National Middle School Association.

Printed in the United States of America

ISBN: 1-56090-065-2

Contents

Acknowledgements

The authors would like to express their appreciation to those persons who made this monograph possible:

— Tammy Paris, Graduate Research Assistant at West Georgia College, who assisted in assembling and reviewing resources and in typing the manuscript.

— John Lounsbury for editing and producing the publication with the assistance of Mary Mitchell in formatting and page layout.

— the researchers, who have greatly increased our understanding of the relationships among parents, families, and schools.

— the practitioners, who have put the research into practice through the implementation of effective family involvement programs which benefit all members of the educational partnership — family, school, and the middle grades student.

J.W.M.
L.M.

Foreword

Out of the extensive discussions and assessments of public education that have been ongoing throughout America in recent years has come a new view on the role of parents and families in education. In some ways this view represents a harkening back to an earlier time, a time when parents kept close tabs on the school activities and assignments of their children and always made a point to meet the teachers personally.

However, the reasons for involving parents and other adults anew in education are not rooted in nostalgia, but rather in necessity. Public awareness of the widely reported inadequacies of education, however valid or invalid, has given rise to a readiness on the part of families to become involved. Then the many studies which collectively might be said to comprise the effective school research data bank have consistently pointed to the involvement of family members as a characteristic of such schools. Students simply learn more in schools where parents take an active part. In addition, those societal changes which have greatly affected the family structure have made the need for such involvement all the more critical.

At the same time those changes which have made parental involvement more desirable have also made it considerably more difficult. Working mothers, one parent families, population mobility, and increased distances between schools and homes because of consolidation are among factors which greatly complicate the development of the desired partnership. So despite the recognized need for and importance of family involvement it is more difficult to achieve.

And if there are special needs for a strong bond between home and school surely they are present at the middle level just as much as at the primary level. The "developmental tasks" involved in the attainment of adolescence are many, and are often traumatic. They are best met with the active assistance of family members and teachers working in concert.

In this essentially new monograph, Drs. John Myers and Louetta Monson have provided a valuable resource to assist in furthering family involvement. It outlines the reasons for encouraging such involvement, identifies some of the roles families may play, provides a comprehensive review of research dealing with family involvement, sets forth guidelines for implementing programs, and lists related resources and organizations. This publication can be and should be put to use immediately.

John Lounsbury
Editor, NMSA Publications

Introduction

When the National Middle School Association published *Involving Parents in Middle Level Education* in 1985, there was relatively little research related to effective parent involvement programs in the middle grades. There was a good deal available concerning the success of parent involvement at the elementary level, but almost nothing had been written about parents and programs above that level. Research into the relationships among parents, families, students, and schools was very limited. The idea of "partnerships" with schools was just emerging.

Today, things have changed. The Family/School Partnership Program, a part of the Fund for the Improvement and Reform of Schools and Teaching set up by the United States Department of Education, has provided funding since 1989 for innovative projects that explore the partnership between home and school. Organizations like the League of Schools Reaching Out, which consists of 41 elementary and middle schools in 19 urban school districts, seek to redefine and expand the role of parent for the schools of tomorrow. Responding to the research of Joyce Epstein, James Comer, and others, school systems are moving rapidly to involve parents and family members in all phases of schooling at all levels.

And finally, it is worth noting that much of the research into families in American society today suggests that "family" or "family member" is a more appropriate term than "parent" for our purposes. The traditional family model does not necessarily apply to some segments of our middle grades student population, especially those considered "at risk." The family situations delineated in J. Howard Johnston's fine NMSA monograph, *The New American Family and the School* (1990), seem to apply best.

Accordingly, we have chosen in this new and completely revised edition to use the terms "family" or "family member," instead of "parent" in our discussion.

We have also provided a greater focus on current research and a more comprehensive listing of references and information resources. It is our hope that this monograph will prove to be of value to middle grades educators seeking greater involvement of family members in school related programs and activities.

Family Members and Middle Grades Programs

When one examines the growing body of research on the involvement of family members in school programs, it is difficult to understand why schools have not done more to utilize these valuable resources. Traditionally, every child who enters the front door of the school has come in with one or more adults who have a strong interest in the child's academic success.

Some years ago, the values within the nuclear family were stronger; they were there to be tapped, but generally the school — particularly at the secondary level — did little to involve parents. In today's changing society the term "parent" does not even adequately reflect the family relationships of many of our children. In *The New American Family and the School,* Johnston (1990) paints a disturbing picture of the "new American family." Almost half of all marriages end in divorce; birthrates have declined. Single-parent families, and family relationships of a non-traditional sort, are on the increase (pp. 3-7). It is no longer accurate to talk of "parent" involvement in schools. In our fluid society, we seek to involve "family members" in support of the educational process. But, because of the changes in the structure of the American family and the blurring of values, our task as educators is even more difficult. Yet, research tells us that the benefits of family involvement in the educational process make it well worth the effort.

Until recently, most research into the involvement of family members in schools focused on the elementary school. Elementary schools have always encouraged family involvement to a much greater degree than secondary schools have. As the research base has grown, schools at all levels are beginning to recognize the significant contribution that interested adults can make to the improvement of learning. The middle school, as a relatively recent innovation, has taken the position that family members are full partners in the educational process. As much as elementary level children, middle graders are in need of caring interaction with and support from parents and family members. The middle level school that does not seek to nurture these relationships is missing a golden opportunity.

Benefits of family involvement

Research in both elementary and middle schools (which will be specifically cited in Chapter 2) has shown clearly several benefits from the involvement of family members in school academic programs. Among these benefits are:

1. Improved student academic performance results from family involvement. Students receive an emotional and motivational boost when family members are actively supporting academic programs. Actions, after all, speak louder than words. The clear message to students at home is that school is important, and non-school adults are willing to invest their time to assure educational quality. Involvement suggests caring. There is evidence that students whose parents or family members are involved with school programs make greater sustained academic gains than students whose parents are not supportive. While all students will benefit from the active involvement of caring adults in school programs, the children whose family members are deeply involved will benefit most.

2. Family members grow closer to their children as school becomes a "family" experience. Family members who interact with middle graders in the school setting as well as at home in relationship to schoolwork gain insights into what makes this age group tick. They come to understand their children better, and the students gain new insights into adult behavior. Both groups are able to share experiences — successes as well as failures.

3. Relationships between home and school, as well as between the school and the community, improve. What goes on at school is no longer a mystery; a child's teacher is no longer just a name. Close cooperation of individuals with the middle level institution builds support in the community as well — support that can prove invaluable in times of crisis, financial or otherwise. Close communication with the community is important to the building of an effective middle grades institution.

4. The variety of skills family members possess help students in the classroom and out, both academically and socially. Adults should not be limited to mundane tasks in the classroom or in other areas; they come to the school with a willingness to help and a repertoire of skills and abilities. They are resources to be tapped. When fully utilized in meaningful ways, adults report that service to children and school is highly rewarding; busy teachers report that family members and adult volunteers often lighten their workloads. It is worth noting that, in an age when people are active into old age, grandparents and other older volunteers represent a valuable, available, and sizable resource for the school. The most effective programs of family and adult volunteer involvement are clearly structured and involve training for teachers and volunteers alike. Teachers must be helped to see the roles that family members can play as partners in the educational process.

5. Students receive all the extra support and understanding they need, both at home and at school. Middle graders face many challenges in our complex society. They are in a time of great physical, psychological, and emotional change. Some are young adults; others in the same classroom are still very much children. No teacher can meet the many needs of each of his or her students, but family members and other adult volunteers can help in providing assistance to individuals. Studies have shown that interactions between children and adults in school settings have a generally positive effect on student behavior and attitudes. In cases where child and parent or family member work in close proximity in the school setting, improvements in individual student behavior may be quite impressive.

6. Adult volunteers save money. It should be obvious that, if adult volunteers have a variety of skills and abilities to offer the school, then some of these services may save the school money. Initially, administrators tend to believe that such savings through a well-organized school volunteer program will tend to be small, but the research concerning volunteer programs suggests the opposite. For example, a county system in rural Tennessee, which had an extensive volunteer program in its schools, calculated how much money it would have cost (at minimum wage) to purchase the services performed by volunteers. It was determined that those services for one school year would have exceeded $275,000.00 (Myers, 1985). Volunteers may prove to be a fine investment. Caring family members, in particular, represent an investment, not only in terms of dollars, but also in terms of family relationships and an understanding of school programs and goals.

In recent years, we have become more aware of the great value of family involvement in middle grades programs. Much of this interest among educational leaders has sprung from the work of a few researchers across the country who are documenting the successes of family and parent involvement in the schools and trying to devise effective models for encouraging such partnerships in learning. In Chapter 2 the work of some leaders in the field is examined.

What Research Says About Family Involvement

Although research on family involvement in schools actually began in the mid-1960s, research specific to the middle level did not appear until the mid-1980s. The results of studies at the elementary level often are applicable to the middle grades as well. According to a National Education Association poll, there is growing public recognition of the importance of family involvement in schools throughout adolescence (Moles, 1982). The increased attention given to this topic in professional literature confirms this opinion.

Unfortunately, the amount of parent and family involvement declines as students progress through the middle and secondary grades (Dauber and Epstein, 1989).

Types of involvement

Several researchers have attempted to identify the major types of parent and family involvement common to American schools. In simplest terms, Moles (1982) recognizes two stages of involvement. The first and more traditional type of involvement is typified by notes sent home to parents and parent conferences. These contacts help parents learn about their children's school performance, and typically suggest ways in which parents and family members can assist.

The second type of participation identified by Moles consists of actual home-learning activities, including home instruction, enrichment activities, parental modeling of educational pursuits, and supervision of homework. Henderson and others (cited in Greenwood and Hickman, 1991) reviewed the literature and found two main areas of participation:

1. activities aimed at supporting the overall school program, and

2. activities aimed at direct assistance to one's own child, such as helping with homework or attending a parent-teacher conference.

Several other researchers have classified parent and family involvement into five or six types. Although the terminology varies, these types include the following roles for parents and family members: 1) teacher of own child, 2) school volunteer, 3) paid paraprofessional, 4) program supporter, 5) learner, 6) audience, and 7) decision maker (Greenwood and Hickman, 1991).

The most frequently mentioned classification model, however, comes from the work of Joyce Epstein (1987). She lists five major types of involvement:

1. **Basic obligations of families** (ensuring children's health and safety; developing skills to prepare children for school; providing supervision, discipline and guidance; and building positive home conditions to support school learning).

2. **Basic obligations of schools** (communication to the home concerning children's progress and school programs).

3. **Involvement in school programs** (parent or family volunteers; attendance at student performances, sporting events, PTA meetings; involvement in school sponsored parent-family education courses).

4. **Involvement in home learning activities coordinated with class work.**

5. **Involvement in school decision-making, governance, or advocacy.**

According to Epstein and Dauber (1991), involvement in home learning activities by family members is a powerful strategy that teachers find useful and parents frequently request. These researchers sum up their findings by stating that:

Schools with programs including the five types of involvement help parents build home conditions for learning, understand communications from the schools, become productive volunteers at school, share responsibilities in their children's education in learning activities related to the curriculum at home, and include parents' voices in decisions that affect the school and their children. There are, literally, hundreds of practices that can be selected to implement each type of involvement. Most practices have not yet been formally evaluated, but the available evidence indicates that the different types of involvement lead to different outcomes for parents, teachers, and students (pp. 291-292).

Parent attitudes and practices

A review of the results of the Tenth Gallup Poll in 1978 concluded that a coordinated effort by teachers and parents is necessary in dealing effectively with problems of discipline, motivation, and development of good work habits at home and school. In that poll, eighty percent of parents with school age children agreed with the idea of having parents attend school one evening per month to learn how to improve children's interest and behavior in school (Gallup, 1978).

The most common way that parents and family members become involved with children's schooling is through homework. Much of the research on parental attitudes toward involvement with schools focuses on their attitudes about homework. In a comparison of elementary and middle level parents, Dauber and Epstein (1989) found that parents of middle level students do not feel as capable of helping their children with homework as do parents of elementary school students. Parents at both levels expressed the belief that they could help their children more if they had guidance from teachers. Typically, parents indicated that they had both the willingness and the time to help their children with school work on weekends, a time when many teachers feel that they are doing families a favor by not assigning homework.

It is important to recognize that indicators of family social class and structure (parents' educational level, family size, marital status) do *not* appear to be associated with parents' ability to help with homework. As might be expected, however, working parents tend to spend less time helping their children with school work than do parents who are not employed outside the home. We also know that, by the middle grades, low achieving students spend less time on homework than do other students. To make matters worse, parents of these low achievers do not offer as much help as do parents of average students. Furthermore, parents of poorer students also receive less information from teachers about how they might help their children (Dauber and Epstein, 1989; Moles, 1982).

Parents who work full or part-time report little involvement at the school site. Other parents report that they would very much like to fill volunteer roles in the school, but have never been asked (Dauber and Epstein, 1989). It is important to note that the attitudes and behaviors of educators, however unintentional, can sometimes alienate parents and family members. Behaviors that school personnel consider "professional" and "businesslike" may be seen by parents and family members as patronizing. Too often, parents report that they feel "talked down to" by teachers and administrators. Parents tend to respond best to educators who approach them with a "personal touch" and treat them as partners in the educational process.

Typically, schools that involve parents and family members as partners in highly relevant and concrete programs (drug education, workshops to help them understand the developmental characteristics of their children, and the like) are generally well supported by parents and families (Lindle, 1989). It is also clear that the level of parent and family involvement in schools is directly linked to a school's practices in informing families about, and assisting them with, their children's education. When teachers actively seek to make parent and family involvement a regular part of their teaching practices, parents increase interaction with their children at home and tend to rate the teachers as better teachers overall (Epstein and Dauber, 1991).

Educators' attitudes and practices

In a National Education Association poll cited in Moles (1982), a large proportion of teachers at all grade levels expressed their strong belief in the value of home-school interaction. According to Useem, as cited by Epstein and Dauber (1991), school programs for involving parents at the elementary level tend to be more comprehensive that those instituted at the middle level.

Middle level teachers use fewer specific communication practices and communicate less often than elementary teachers with fewer individual families. Middle grades parents receive less information or guidance at the very time they need more information and more guidance in how to be involved in larger and more complex class schedules and subjects (p. 300).

Because teachers in self-contained classes have fewer students than those in departmentalized or teamed situations, they tend to make more frequent contacts with parents (Epstein and Dauber, 1991). Teachers of language arts emphasize the desirability of involving parents, and tend to implement practices to do so more than teachers of other academic subjects, They focus particularly on helping parents and family members become more involved in various learning activities at home. Unfortunately, research tells us that teachers of mathematics, science, and social studies are less supportive of practices aimed at encouraging parent and family participation (Epstein and Dauber, 1991).

Teacher personality characteristics also have an impact on success in parent and family involvement programs. In a study by Hoover-Dempsey, Bassler, and Brissie, cited in Greenwood and Hickman (1991), teacher efficacy, or teachers' beliefs in their own teaching effectiveness, was a strong predictor of teacher success in involving parents in school programs. Teachers who successfully implemented involvement programs tended to avoid making stereotypical judgments about the capabilities and willingness to participate of single, socio-economically disadvantaged, or less educated parents. Typically, teachers who were successful at

involving parents, rated all types of parents high on helpfulness —
regardless of the qualifications they brought to the role. (Epstein
and Dauber, 1991). According to the same study,

> Teachers with more positive attitudes toward par-
> ent involvement place more importance than other
> teachers on such practices as holding conferences with
> all students' parents, communicating with parents
> about school programs, and providing parents both
> good and bad reports about students' progress. More
> positive attitudes also are positively correlated with
> more success in involving 'hard to reach' parents...

If teachers do not believe that parents are interested in
being involved, they make fewer efforts to involve them. When
teachers share common beliefs about parent and family involvement with administrators and colleagues, they tend to have
stronger involvement practices.

In a synthesis of research, Moles (1982) discovered that
many programs use individual conferences, workshops, home
visits, or telephone calls to involve parents and family members.
Interestingly, most programs that he identified had improved
achievement in mathematics and reading as major goals. More
than half were also concerned with social development and
improving school attendance. Although many studies have ac-
knowledged the value of parent and family involvement, Greenwood and Hickman (1991) noted that there is little emphasis on
this issue in American teacher education programs. Teachers and
administrators receive very little — if any — training in methods
for effectively involving parents and family members in schools.

Barriers to parent and family involvement

Barriers which discourage parent and family involvement
in school programs tend to fall into three major categories. The
first involves the attitudes and abilities of parents and family
members. Many adults perceive school as a "negative" place,
based on memories of their own unpleasant experiences. This is

exacerbated by messages from the school, which in many cases tend to be "negative" as well. As a result, many adults do not see the school as a positive, warm, and caring place for their children (Greenwood and Hickman, 1991; Moles, 1982). To quote Greenwood and Hickman, "Some parents do not value education; others feel powerless to influence the school. Still others may believe that running schools should be 'left up to the experts'" (p. 282). Especially in the middle grades, parents may feel that academic school work is beyond their ability to provide assistance.

The second category of barriers relates to the work schedule, health status, and conflicting family commitments of those parents who might become involved. Moles (1982) cites research by Leitch and Tangri, who identified "work and poor health" as two main reasons given by parents for not participating in school programs. Policies in the work place that do not allow parents to leave work to participate in school programs were identified by Espinoza, cited in Greenwood and Hickman (1991), as a major deterrent to family involvement. According to Leitch and Tangri, having small children at home and receiving late notice of meetings and activities are additional deterrents cited by parents. They also reported that, in many communities, both teachers and family members reported fears for their personal safety when attending evening school activities.

The third category of barriers to involvement relates to the knowledge, attitudes, and skill levels of teachers and administrators. Teachers also have responsibilities at home that compete with school commitments. Teachers also report feeling overwhelmed by the problems in the lives of students and their families (Leitch and Tangri, as cited in Moles, 1982). Williams and Stallworth, cited in Greenwood and Hickman (1991), found that principals and teachers generally prefer the traditional parent roles — such as assisting with fundraisers. Apparently, there is some risk perceived in making families full partners in the educational process.

Williams and Chavkin, cited in Greenwood and Hickman (1991), identified seven essential elements for overcoming barriers and developing involvement programs. These are: 1) written policies, 2) administrative support, 3) training, 4) a partnership approach, 5) two-way communication, 6) networking, and 7) evaluation.

Effects of parent and family involvement

Studies show that the value of education is impressed upon students when they see their parents and other family members actively involved in support of the school program. Several studies cited by Greenwood and Hickman (1991) document the benefits of successful family involvement. These positive effects include:

1. higher achievement,
2. improved school attendance,
3. improved student sense of well-being,
4. improved student behavior,
5. better parent and student perceptions of classroom and school climate,
6. better student readiness to complete homework,
7. higher educational aspirations among students and parents,
8. better student grades,
9. increased educational productivity of time that parents and children spend together, and
10. greater parent satisfaction with teachers.

Obviously, with the power of parent and family involvement to positively influence the success with which schools accomplish their missions, it is definitely worth the time and effort of school personnel to dedicate extensive resources to develop effective involvement programs. In the next chapter, specific ways in which the school might utilize family members as partners in the educational process will be examined.

What Families Have to Offer the Middle Grades

Parents and other family members have a wide variety of interests and abilities that can be of great value to individual students and to middle level programs. In a very real sense, family members can do virtually anything that needs doing. Data are emerging every day to document the positive benefits that family support and assistance can have on student attitude and achievement.

Teachers have long felt that students who had strong support from their family members did better in school. Now data support that hunch. Just as family involvement can work wonders for the individual child, it can also have a powerful impact on school programs. Families are rich in volunteer resources.

Over the past two decades, data have been compiled by successful school volunteer programs across the nation to demonstrate that parents, grandparents, and other volunteers are often a vast but neglected resource, a resource that can address virtually any educational need. The hard part, of course, is finding the volunteers with the particular skills needed and matching them to the jobs that need doing. Theoretically, there is *nothing* that family members cannot do. "Wait just a minute," you say, "a parent is not a certified classroom teacher, and cannot be given the responsibilities of a teacher." However, you might be surprised at how many adults there are in your school community who are non-practicing, but fully certified teachers. In one case, where a qualified substitute could not be found for a fifth grade classroom while the regular teacher took an extended leave, the principal approached a parent, a former elementary teacher, and convinced her to rejoin the profession for a few months. You may not realize the resources available to you until you look. In the case cited, the administrator recognized that families can be full partners in the educational process. He took the time to learn something about the talents residing in his school's families. When the need arose, he knew where to turn to augment his list of substitutes.

It is worth noting that one of the most neglected family roles in most schools is that of "learner." Family volunteers are usually good learners and can be taught to meet specific school needs, from how to operate the computer in the office to how to conduct vision screening for students. Parents and other adult family members come with a wealth of experience and skills upon which the school can build. The list of what family members have to offer is extensive. A few suggested roles are given below.

1. Instructional roles. While the number of family members with formal teaching credentials may be few, virtually every adult has something of value to share from his or her experiences. A parent with skills in photography or dance might enter the instructional program as a guest instructor, as a source of support materials for a specific teaching unit, or as an assistant in a mini-course.

Adults involved in the workplace can provide new insights into topics covered in the middle level classroom. Family members employed in the health professions may add a new dimension to classroom instruction related to drug or sex education. Those employed in business and industry may provide interesting sites for field trips — from a working cattle farm to a television station. Family members can also be contacts — open doors — to other businesses, agencies, and institutions in the community. Networking is always to be encouraged. Many adults pursue interesting hobbies and would be only too happy to share the information with students. All you have to do is ask. You might even find someone so devoted to their avocation that they are willing to take a leadership role in getting something started in your school; an adviser for a new club, or an assistant for the intramural program, might be waiting for an invitation to serve. Family members can also make a strong impact as tutors, working to challenge advanced students or providing individual attention others might need. Sometimes, in the area of curriculum planning, an outsider may have the clearest view; a family member might even serve as a planner, as a temporary member of an instructional team.

2. Instructional support roles (non-teaching). We often hear the complaint that there are just too many non-teaching responsibilities for teachers these days. Anyone who has taught more than one week in a public school will recognize the validity of that assertion. Teachers are busy people — no doubt about it — but many of their non-teaching activities could be carried out by volunteers, coming either from families or through a formal school volunteer program.

Family members in direct support of instruction can develop and evaluate instructional materials; they can take charge of classroom bulletin boards. With guidance, they can type, file papers, collect monies, make copies, and assist with the myriad other tasks that middle level teachers pursue. Parents and other adults can arrange for and chaperone field trips. A motivated adult volunteer could locate, evaluate, and prepare audio-visual materials for classroom use. Volunteers can serve as "home base" assistants. In short, family members and other adult volunteers can relieve teachers of much of the "administrivia" associated with teaching.

3. Other roles. Family members might also serve as:

— audience for student presentations, at the classroom, team, or school-wide level.

—aides to the librarian, the office staff, the counselor, the school nurse, the cafeteria staff, or the maintenance staff.

—coordinators for a formal school volunteer program. The principal and teachers need not be burdened with the day-to-day operation of such a program. Experience shows that programs with coordinators tend to be more effective than those where coordination is an "extra duty" for a teacher or administrator.

—members of school-wide committees, dealing with everything from curricular change to the hiring of new staff members. If family members are to become full-fledged members of the home-school partnership, then they must also be involved in the formation of policy and procedures at a school-wide level.

—special projects committee members, handling such major activities as the annual spring carnival, raising funds for playground renovation, and other major and minor roles.

—maintenance and custodial assistants, especially in support of special projects. This type involvement was dramatically demonstrated by a rural middle school in Tennessee, where a group of parents noted the need for a new air conditioning system, raised the money for it, then installed it themselves. While assisting with special maintenance and custodial projects is not a very glamorous volunteer role, it is an important one, and in every community there are people who would welcome the opportunity to contribute in this way.

—recruiters of other volunteers. One lesson learned from the school volunteer movement is that the best way to recruit is "each one get one." The personal touch is most effective, when one volunteer says to another, "Come and join me." When a family member or other volunteer is "hooked" on being involved in the middle school program, he or she is your best salesperson for attracting other volunteers.

Regardless of the roles they fill, when dealing with adults assisting with school programs, it is worth remembering that they are *learners* and that they can be utilized to do virtually *anything*. Become aware of what family members and other adult volunteers can offer the school and consider what the school can offer them.

The Importance of
Good Communication

Successful family involvement programs require clear lines of communication between family and school. Indeed, the first step in developing and implementing any sort of comprehensive family involvement program is to establish clear and varied means of communication between school and home. Partnerships in learning are much like a marriage; without open lines of communications between the partners, the relationship is likely to disintegrate. Involvement of family members will tend to improve communication between home and school, but there must be some lines of open communication in place at the outset. Families must understand what the school is about, and must have the means for expressing their concerns to school authorities; likewise the school must understand what is happening in the home and community. This bond of mutual communication and understanding is the base upon which a successful family involvement program must be built.

A communication bond usually exists in the early grades via active parent-teacher organizations, homeroom mothers, regular conferences, and a variety of other joint activities The junior high school model, however, tended to follow the lead of the high school which often minimized the roles of parents and family members in the academic program. Indeed, teachers and family members have been conditioned to feel ill at ease in one another's presence in the middle grades and above. If you doubt the truth of this assertion, talk with parents and teachers of children in the upper grades. Better yet, if you have children in these grades, get permission to spend a day shadowing your child; sit in classes, and observe the verbal and non-verbal reactions you elicit. Historically, in the upper grades, family members are most often invited to school when there is an academic or behavioral problem with the child. The point is that, in the middle grades, you are likely to have to educate families as to their role before you can involve them willingly in the educational process. Families must come to understand that they have a right and a responsibility to be fully involved in the education of their children. This process of expanding their role in education begins with the establishment of clear lines of communication.

Ways to communicate with families

There are numerous ways to communicate, but the following should prove most effective:

1. Build and maintain a strong family-school (parent-teacher) organization, and be sure that "family" is interpreted in a broad sense. The old PTA or PTO model still works, but it might best be called an FSA or FSO, reflecting that not only teachers and parents are welcome. A dynamic organization will involve teachers, administrators, counselors and other school staff, as well as parents, guardians, older siblings, and other members of the larger family. Many family members come to you with a strong history of involvement in some sort of organization at the elementary level. Seize the moment, even before the children arrive at your school, to make it known that there are roles for family members, and that families are expected to play a part in the child's schooling. Family-school organizations that have no real role in the business of schooling, that only exist to run the annual carnival, are a waste of valuable resources. An effective FSA or FSO must be involved in all facets of the school program, and it requires the full support of teachers and administrators to function optimally.

2. Implement an "open door" policy. In an effective middle school, teachers and administrators are accessible to family members; in turn, family members who are treated with courtesy, understanding, and tact will not abuse the privilege. Administrators and teachers must be willing to listen to what family members have to say, and weigh comments as one would the advice of a business partner. It is sad that in many schools face to face discussion between home and school occurs only when there is a problem with the child. Rarely does a family member stop by to offer a fund-raising suggestion or suggest an idea for a field trip. Traditionally, the breadth of topics for discussion between home and school has been somewhat narrow.

3. Establish a school newsletter that goes home by regular mail at least quarterly. Devise a catchy title, and fill the newsletter with the good things that are going on at school. Recognize student achievements, but also note accomplishments of teachers, staff, and families. Build linkages to a broader community. Remind families about upcoming events; include a "From the principal..." column. Tell your families what the school needs to continue doing the best job possible for their children. Ask for volunteers. The newsletter could be a joint venture of the school and the family-school organization.

If you already have formal programs which involve family members or other volunteers, consider doing a quarterly newsletter reflecting that service. Such amenities make volunteers feel special, and provide high program visibility. Another option would be to have a "volunteer" or "service" insert for the regular newsletter. If you have a coordinator for volunteer services, production of such a specialized newsletter should be part of that person's responsibility.

4. Start off right by involving family members in the orientation process. Consider sending families formal letters of invitation to a spring orientation. The traditional "open house" several weeks after school has opened is too little and too late. A full-fledged orientation program for family members involves home mailings, well planned formal orientation programs, and provision for follow-up contacts. Consider something like a pancake breakfast, or week-end barbecue — some special social event — for new students and families. Such an event would be a great opportunity for sponsorship by the family-school association and a chance to recruit new parents.

5. Encourage personal notes and telephone calls by teachers to homes. Provide each teacher with attractive note paper, and strongly urge its use. Some schools have found pre-stamped post-cards quite effective, since it is relatively easy for a teacher to pick one up, write a quick note, and mail it. Encourage teachers to call parents to report student successes, not just in times of crisis. Bearers of good news put themselves in a good position to ask for family assistance for class projects later on. Too many teachers contact the home only in times of trouble, claiming that they are "too busy" to call at other times. It is easy to "pass the buck" to the principal or counselor in bad times, and to ignore the good. Actually, the time spent building viable partnerships can save teacher time later on. Good relationships with family members can yield dividends for teachers, students, and school. After all, how can we have a partnership, if the partners never communicate with one another?

6. Mail special materials home. Many professional associations (for example, the National Middle School Association, the National Council of Teachers of English, and the International Reading Association) offer a variety of helpful flyers and booklets that are inexpensive and suitable for mailing to families. There are flyers that suggest how the family can help the child develop better study and reading skills. There are materials that explain what a middle school is, and others deal with career awareness, nutrition, and other relevant topics. The school can become a small clearinghouse for materials that can educate family members in areas beyond the traditional academic curriculum. With the marvels of desktop publishing, schools can also develop their own materials, fliers about upcoming events or ones designed to help recruit volunteers for school projects. Along with a regular newsletter, such mailings keep the school highly visible to families. Regular periodic mailings is a proven marketing technique with endless variations.

7. Conduct special events during the year. Enlist the help of the family-school organization and other volunteers to plan the school carnival, but also plan several other activities as well. One or two big events per year are simply not sufficient. Consider weekend activities that will draw the family as a unit. Some schools have had good success with a weekly or monthly pancake breakfast that encourages working parents to come to school with the child one morning before going to work. Such programs get family members into the school, giving you a captive audience. Make the best use of your family-school organization meetings as well; use them to educate. A strong organization, with relevant programs, will encourage family members and teachers to attend — and to get further involved.

8. Conduct surveys to determine family members' skills and qualifications. Develop a short survey instrument that can be used as part of the orientation process, filled out at a school event, or mailed home. Find out what family members do for a living, what their hobbies are, and whether or not they would be willing to donate time or their skills to the school. Find out who has teacher certification or other applicable experience and training. Locate those with experience coaching in community sports programs. Compiling such a database will enable you to pinpoint your resources. The family member who sells widgets during the day may be a skilled photographer or artist at night. Such people make great classroom resources. But you are not likely to learn what resources are available, unless you survey to find them.

9. Set up a "welcome wagon" to greet new arrivals during the school year. Family volunteers are perfect for such a role. This might also be a project of the family-school organization. They can visit the home and personally orient the new family to the school and the community. Personal contact by the principal, or the child's teacher-advisor, is also appropriate. Most families who receive a warm welcome to a new school and community will see it as an invitation to become further involved.

10. Encourage the use of "telephone chains" to put a personal touch in spreading news. Again, the family-school organization can be of great help. If a team is planning something and wants to invite the parents, each team member can call one and start up the previously planned telephone tree. The same principle works equally well on a school-wide basis.

11. Publish a calendar of events. One that is suitable for posting at home on the refrigerator early in the year is preferable. Once again, desktop publishing enables us to produce print shop quality calendars with minimal effort. If families know well in advance that an event is coming, and if they are reminded at the appropriate time, they are more likely to attend. Little slips of dittoed paper that are given to students to take home one week before the family-school organization meeting are not going to boost attendance.

A fine wall calendar, imprinted with major school events, makes an excellent fund-raiser as well as a communication device. Most families keep some kind of calendar posted somewhere in their home; a school calendar would be a daily reminder to express the importance of a good education. One school developed an excellent fund-raiser for the student council by selling calendars that featured pen and ink drawings of local sites of interest that were done by students. The calendars sold well. Unlike some fund raising items, these were practical. Considering the cost of "designer" calendars from the local card or gift shop, school calendar sales can be an effective fund raising activity, and another tool for effective communication.

Once multiple lines of communication are in place, the foundation is prepared for the development of effective involvement programs.

Implementing Family Involvement Programs

The most effective way to involve families in middle level programs is to give top priority to this task and start a formal program. While the family and child will benefit from any involvement, from the school's perspective, the greatest gain is likely to come from a well-planned program that involves both families and volunteers from the larger community. Such programs can meet virtually any school need — fund raising or service — and can often save the school money by meeting needs that otherwise might be paid out of the school's limited funds.

Most volunteers are primarily focused on meeting the needs of their own children. There are, however, great numbers of persons in families and communities who are willing to give of their time and resources for the good of schools and children in general. A formal volunteer program allows the school to tap into these resources, as well those available through families.

Establishing an effective program

Establishing an effective program is probably best done by following the ten steps below.

Step 1. Begin with a needs assessment. First, find out exactly what needs — academic, physical, and others — exist. Survey teachers; seek ideas from families and community members. Ask students; ask the librarian, the janitor, the cafeteria staff. Just being consulted will make them all feel more like members of a community, ones whose opinions are valued. In order to secure a full range of suggestions, you may first have to convince them that volunteers can do just about anything. Make a strong effort to develop a valid and extensive list of needs. It doesn't really matter whether the need affects the entire school, or only a single teacher in his or her classroom. It all begins with a widespread assessment of needs.

Step 2. While the needs assessment is underway — if not before — select a program coordinator. The principal should not assume the role of "coordinator" as an additional duty, and the same holds true for most members of the staff and faculty. When assigned to a teacher as an "additional" duty, family and community involvement programs soon cease to have priority. The principal always needs to be leading the way, but he or she will not have the time required to coordinate the activities of a dynamic volunteer program. Experience has shown a direct relationship between the quality of a program and the dedication of the coordinator. The coordinator is the key person who makes it all happen. The individual selected should be a dynamic, committed individual, with good interpersonal skills and strong dedication to the program. The larger the program, the greater the need for a competent person who has the time, skills, interest, and dedication to make the program successful.

The possibility of providing some monetary compensation for the coordinator should be explored fully. Even a small salary tends to generate a sense of commitment. A budget administered by the coordinator will also build a sense of responsibility. Often, programs coordinated by persons who are themselves unpaid volunteers with no fiscal responsibilities in the program come to be viewed casually; responsibility and compensation ensure a businesslike approach to coordination. Many fine volunteer programs in individual middle schools are coordinated by unpaid, part-time volunteers — usually parents — who possess the skills and experience to succeed in that role. It takes, however, a very dedicated person to serve for the long term in such a demanding role without some recompense.

If no funds are available to pay a program coordinator, you will have to begin with an enthusiastic volunteer. If you have conducted a thorough survey of skills and experiences of family members, and you have a strong and active family-school organization, you should not have to look far to find a suitable candidate.

If you cannot find an individual willing to assume the role, consider appointing co-coordinators. Often, two volunteers will undertake what neither would attempt alone. Responsibilities can be divided and each coordinator can provide moral support for the other.

Although the decision on the appointment should be made by the principal, it is recommended that nominations be made from a committee of teachers and family representatives. Shared decision-making results in a shared sense of responsibility to support the coordinator as the program gets underway. Once you have located a coordinator, it is the responsibility of the principal to make the new coordinator's job as important and pleasant as possible.

Step 3. Once the coordinator is in place and the needs assessment has been completed, the time has come to match needs and resources. If a survey of family members' experience, skills, and qualifications has not already been done, now is the time. The principal should convene a committee composed of both faculty and family representatives to prioritize identified needs and allot identified resources. Needs that cannot be met by identified resources among family members might be met by soliciting volunteers from the larger community. The newly appointed coordinator should have a major role in this entire process.

Step 4. The fourth step is an important one — the education of teachers and other school personnel as to the value of family and community volunteers in the school program. This process began earlier and needs to be successfully completed if the program is to thrive; faculty and staff support just must be there. Unfortunately, experience has shown that teachers are quite often reluctant to utilize a volunteer; they do not always see the many ways in which a volunteer can help. At first thought, many teachers perceive that volunteers in the classroom or school will be a "bother," and they may even see them as intruders. Some teachers will initially be uneasy with family members in the classrooms "watching me teach." Others will say that they do not have the time to plan work for the volunteer, or that they do not know how to utilize a volunteer. Both of these assertions are usually true. Middle level teachers are busy folks, and they have not been trained to use volunteers.

It is the responsibility of both the principal and the coordinator to work with the faculty and staff to show them how extra pairs of hands can be a boon to their busy schedules. Time invested in developing an appreciation of volunteer roles in the classroom will reap handsome rewards in terms of time saved in the long run. Helping teachers to see the value of volunteer help really is not difficult. Most teachers want help, and most see an educational partnership, especially with family members, as a desirable thing. It's just a new idea to them; they need a bit of guidance and some time to reflect on the idea before buying in.

A well-prepared coordinator can discuss the volunteer program at general in-service or departmental meetings, can distribute materials on the positive effects of volunteer partnerships, and can visit classrooms to help individual teachers identify specific needs. The coordinator must be prepared to market the program to the faculty on a continuing basis.

Ideally in time, teachers will come to the coordinator with needs and ideas for program improvement, viewing the program as a valuable addition to the larger educational program. The coordinator can assess the degree of "teacher education" needed by analyzing the results of the teacher portion of the needs assessment done in step one. If responses were limited, then more preparation is probably required.

In most cases, the needs assessment will yield an ample number of ways in which teachers believe they might utilize volunteers. Middle level teachers normally recognize a "good deal" when they see it, and — in most cases — teacher education should not require the "hard sell." Rather, it should be an opportunity for the coordinator to guide the teacher in expanding the list of possible volunteer roles, and to discuss the nuts and bolts of working with classroom volunteers. The selling of the concept and program to faculty and staff is, however, essential to program success. A program that is not supported by the faculty will not endure and will never achieve its full potential. Once launched, however, a dynamic program supported by the majority of faculty and staff will sell itself. Teachers should not be forced to utilize volunteers; a good program will let them *want* to become educational partners.

Step 5. With needs and resources matched and the coordinator in place, the administrative routine of program operation should begin to fall into place as well. While the coordinator and principal are preparing teachers and working out operational details, the coordinator should begin the fifth step of the process, the recruitment of volunteers. If individuals have been identified earlier in the process, then direct contact is appropriate. A telephone call is probably the most effective means of initial contact. Through newsletters or community news stories, families and communities should already be aware that the school is initiating a comprehensive volunteer program. Accordingly, a call from the coordinator should not come as a great surprise.

Before committing a parent to the program, however, it is essential that the volunteer also meet certain criteria. It is not enough for the person simply to have some skills needed by the school; the volunteer should also be someone caring and reliable, who relates well to children. To assess such nebulous qualities a personal interview is in order. Unfortunately there are family and community members who want to work with schools and children for the wrong reasons.

Accordingly, care must be taken in recruitment. All persons who are to work in the school should, ideally, be interviewed by the coordinator. This need not, however, be a lengthy or complex process. The particular volunteer role will often dictate what depth is required. Certainly a parent active in the family-school organization requires less screening than a community member who walks in off the street to volunteer. It is advisable to utilize some simple application form; for some roles, it is also appropriate to request the names of references. While such procedures may seem stringent for a small school and community, they are essential for large programs. Regardless of school size or location, some screening process should always be in place. Criteria that would assist in weeding out those who should not be involved are needed.

If no one has been identified to meet a particular need, then the coordinator must work through the family-school organization, through home mailings, or other contacts to recruit. Preference is usually given to family members as they have a stronger vested interest in school programs than do general community members. One group often neglected as a resource is grandparents. They usually have more time available than other family members, have more experience in living, and can provide the opportunities middle level students need to participate in intergenerational experiences. Older adults are often the best volunteers, for a variety of reasons.

Generally speaking, the best recruiting technique is "each one gets one." Current volunteers are your best source of future volunteers. Each volunteer has friends, family members, co-workers with skills that the school may need. If volunteers enjoy their roles, their enthusiasm will spread to others. This seems particularly true among older volunteers as a group. Working with children in schools often provides a new focus for valuing life for someone who is no longer a member of the regular workforce. These people like to talk about the children and their volunteer role. Their enthusiasm is contagious.

Whatever procedures are developed for recruitment and screening, the important thing is to get the right people active in the program, people who care about education and children, people who want to be partners in the exciting process of middle level education.

Step 6. Once volunteers have been recruited, the next step is to orient them and provide needed training. You cannot expect volunteers to "fit right in." Some may be able to do so, but for most the middle school will be a foreign environment. They will need help adapting. Most adult volunteers have been out of school for years, and their only insight into middle level education may be based on their own junior high school experience. They are more likely to think of education in terms of the traditional secondary school model; team planning, advisor-advisee, flexible scheduling, and other facets common to the middle school will seem strange to them. Volunteers need to be oriented to middle level philosophy and how it is practiced in your school. They also need to understand day-to-day school operation. This can be accomplished by the coordinator through written materials, locally produced video materials, volunteer handbooks, and visits in the school along with discussions.

While orienting new volunteers, the coordinator will also have the opportunity to learn more about them as individuals. This will enable the coordinator to make a better match in placing volunteers. The perfect placement results in a volunteer who loves his or her role and has a fine working rapport with the faculty or staff supervisor. Human differences being what they are, not all people work well together. Through experience, the coordinator will develop a knack for making proper placements. Once a placement is made, the coordinator assists the faculty or staff supervisor as needed in providing any additional training required for the volunteer role. And remember, a good volunteer can be trained to do virtually *anything* that needs doing.

Step 7. Now that the volunteers are trained and placed, the real coordination process begins. The coordinator must continuously assess the program and make adjustments. The coordinator needs to visit classrooms and other work sites on a regular basis. Sometimes needs change; sometimes people change. In any event, it is the coordinator's business to know how things are going. Since some volunteers will be lost through natural attrition —health problems, relocation, employment, and the like — the coordinator must also continue to build a pool from which to recruit new volunteers. This is where the communications network plays a major role. Through newsletters, regular in-service meetings with volunteers, and other means, the coordinator needs to maintain strong lines of communication. Once volunteers are settled in roles at various worksites, it is easy to lose touch. Effective communication networks require maintenance.

Step 8. One major role of the coordinator is to provide recognition for those persons who help with school needs, as well as for the faculty and staff who utilize them. A "thank you" banquet at the end of the year is a fine idea, but it should not stand alone. Recognition should be ongoing. Building morale is a continuous responsibility for the coordinator. In addition, teachers need to let volunteers know when they are doing a good job. At the same time, it should be said that volunteers need to let faculty and staff supervisors know that they value and enjoy their roles.

The coordinator can nurture the process of recognition in a variety of ways. Letters or cards of appreciation are always appreciated. Personal notes from the principal are excellent ways to recognize some superior service or accomplishment. Feature articles in the newsletter or radio spots are very much in order. A creative coordinator will develop innovative ways to recognize people. Sometimes, the right word at the right time is all that's needed.

Step 9. At the same time that the coordinator is maintaining morale, he or she should also work to keep the volunteer program a "high profile" in the community. Articles in the local newspapers or media coverage of school events and activities that involve volunteers are effective public relations techniques. Publishing a program newsletter that is widely distributed is another. Recruiting flyers and a volunteer "handbook" also keep the program before the public eye, if they are disseminated widely in appropriate places. Doctors' and dentists' offices are good places to place materials. They can also be mailed as a courtesy to board members, as well as to community leaders and business organizations. Such efforts may result in new volunteers, or other forms of support. Some schools have approached local businesses with requests for direct support of school volunteer programs with excellent results, both in terms of funding and personnel. There are cases where major corporations have released personnel on company time to perform services for schools. Many businesses have "adopted" school events and activities, providing funds and other support. The volunteer program can be a component in the increasing number of school-business partnerships that are now emerging.

Step 10. The final step is to conduct regular formal evaluation of the program. It is important for volunteer programs to justify their existence to the school and community. Therefore, an evaluation process is important, since it provides educational "accountability." With input from the principal and others, the coordinator should develop criteria for program evaluation, and issue an extensive written annual report that includes demographic data on volunteers, projects supported, special accomplishments, and other supportive information. While general positive evaluations of participants are helpful, specific and objective data look better to a school board considering requests for next year's funding. It is worthwhile to record the number of volunteer hours donated and, using current minimum wage figures, compute how much money the school would have had to spend to receive the same services. A comprehensive, professional annual report will justify a request for an expanded program budget. Such a report may be literally worth its weight in gold.

If the volunteer program in your school consists only of a few family members helping in the library and one or two classrooms, you may want to think bigger. Limited family involvement is a start toward a comprehensive volunteer program that can provide a myriad of free services — from tutoring to dental screening — for middle level students. In tight budgetary times, a program that may be worth money is certainly worth thinking about.

| Programs That Work

In the early 1980s, while surveying the literature in connection with *Involving Parents in Middle Level Education,* it was difficult to find any mention of parent or family involvement programs in the middle grades. A number of elementary school programs had been profiled in the literature, but information about effective middle grades and secondary level programs was nearly non-existent. A decade later, the situation has changed and middle level programs of various sorts have appeared from coast to coast as a part of the expanded attention that family involvement is now receiving. Indeed, the October 1989 issue of *Educational Leadership* was subtitled "strengthening partnerships with parents and community," and several articles focused on trends related to family involvement.

In that issue information could be found on the following four programs: 1) Project TEACH in Kanawha County, West Virginia, which frees teachers for computer training by providing released time for business people to come into the schools and teach real-world skills and facilitate other school activities (Merenda, 1989); 2) the Albuquerque Public Schools Parent Center, which trained pre-service and in-service teachers to utilize family volunteers; 3) the program at Tierra Amarillo, New Mexico, that provided released time for central office administrative staff to serve one day per month as school volunteers; and 4) the program at Las Lunas, New Mexico, which involved family members in system-wide curriculum planning (Williams and Chavkin, 1989).

These programs are examples of the trends toward involving various groups within the community as school volunteers. In recent years, business-school partnerships have become popular;

while often involving monetary support, many programs also provide released time for employees to work with school activities and projects. Because of the research that has appeared related to parent involvement, the need for volunteer training has become an established part of volunteer programs as well. Technology has also left its imprint. The Trans*Parent* program implemented in Lawrence Middle School in Nashville, Tennessee, sought to build closer links between teacher and family through the use of computer and advanced communications technology (Bauch, 1989). In the years ahead, supported by reports like that of the Carnegie Corporation's Commission on Adolescent Development, *Turning Points: Preparing American Youth for the 21st Century* (1989), involvement of parents and family members in middle level programs — in various roles — can be expected to grow rapidly. Accordingly, information on successful program models will become even more accessible.

What is new in the 1990s related to parent and family involvement is the interest of federal and state agencies. In addition to the Family/School Partnership Program sponsored by the U.S. Department of Education and programs sponsored by organizations like the League of Schools Reaching Out, a number of states have launched state-wide initiatives. In 1986, the Tennessee General Assembly appropriated $1,000,000 for the development of 11 parent involvement models at 17 sites across the state (Lueder, 1989). The efforts to improve parent and family involvement at Emerson Elementary School in Rosemead, California were encouraged by passage of a California State Board of Education policy aimed at ensuring family-school partnership in the educational process (Davis, 1989). More recently, several states have fielded strong programs that encourage interaction and dynamic partnerships between family and school. Two leading states in this national trend have been Florida and Wisconsin.

The Red Carpet Schools Program

Initiated in 1989 as a joint project of the Sunshine State School Public Relations Association and the Florida Department of Education, the Red Carpet Schools Program aims at encouraging greater family-school involvement. It encourages schools in the state to become more "parent/family friendly" through an extensive program of recognition. Schools selected as "Red Carpet Schools" receive a letter of congratulations from the Commissioner of Education, a certificate of recognition, window decal, and a large red "Red Carpet" floor mat for the front door. Appropriate ceremonies are held. Upon request, the school may borrow a large red banner from the state department, and other "Red Carpet" items are available from private vendors. The selection criteria insure that only schools with a strong family involvement program can be recognized. Schools may only be nominated by a parent-family group from within the school. The helpful attitudes of principal and staff, provisions for parent education programs, family involvement in the academic process, and the degree of communications between family and school are considerations. The program is run at the district level, with ample materials and support from the State Department of Education.

In 1990, the second phase of the Red Carpet Schools Program went into effect. Called "Home is a School Zone Too," this second phase focuses on involvement of family members in the education process itself. As part of this campaign, the Department of Education fielded a 74 page "Family Recruitment Campaign Notebook" packed with ideas and information, models and methods for enhancing parent and family involvement at the school level. The program places an emphasis on training teachers and staff to work with family members in productive roles in support of the educational process. Further information on the Florida Initiative is available from the Office of Business and Citizen Partnerships, Florida Department of Education, 126 Florida Education Center, Tallahassee, FL 32399-0400.(904) 488-8385.

The Families in Education Program

This project, sponsored by the Wisconsin Department of Public Instruction, grew out of the state proclaimed "Year of the Family in Education" started in 1987. The goals of that initiative were to develop a sense of cooperative responsibility among schools and parents, to develop programs that would encourage such partnerships in the solution of both academic and non-academic problems facing the schools, to enhance positive communication among all partners, and to develop a greater understanding in the community of the value that parents and family members lend to the educational process. In 1987, an advisory committee was formed and a packet of materials, stressing "monthly themes" was provided to each school district. The monthly theme approach ensured that parent-family involvement remained a high visibility goal all year long.

Over the course of the year, administrative conferences focused on parent-family involvement. The annual fall conference for district administrators heard from Joyce Epstein, a nationally recognized expert on family involvement. The legislature made grant monies available to local governmental units and school districts. A comprehensive public relations program was "kicked off" during a Green Bay Packers game. Newsletters were published, community forums were held, "Family in Education Day" was proclaimed by the State Assembly. Plans were laid for the development of informational brochures, an Educator's Resource Handbook, and a Family Involvement Resource and Planning Guide.

In 1989, the program expanded its scope with the appointment of a task force on early education, child care, and family involvement. The 1989-91 biennial budget included funding for "learning assistance grants" to help school districts develop collaborative health and social service programs for students and families. The 1989-90 year was designated the "Year of Community Partnerships," seeking to expand the partnerships begun with families to the greater community.

In support of these programs, the State Department of Public Instruction has fielded an extensive series of effective theme packets, which are available for a reasonable fee through their publications office (800-243-8782). Additional information on the program is available from the Families in Education Program, Wisconsin Department of Public Instruction, P.O. Box 7841, Madison, WI 53707-7841. (608) 266-9757.

| Resources

Professional literature has greatly expanded in its coverage of family involvement. Listed below is a portion of such references which will serve as sources for additional information.

Following that list are a surprising number of organizations and associations that are involved with aspects of family involvement in education.

Articles, Reports, and Monographs

Alper, C. et al. (1982). People are your most valuable resources. *Instructor, 92,* 42-44.

Bauch, J. (1989). The Trans*Parent* school model: New technology for parent involvement. *Educational Leadership, 47*(2), 32-34.

Bingham, A. (1982). Writing newsletters for parents. *Language Arts, 59,* 445- 450.

Brandt, R. (1989). On parents and schools: A conversation with Joyce Epstein. *Educational Leadership, 47*(2), 24-27.

Cervone, B., & O'Leary, K. (1982). A conceptual framework for parent involvement. *Educational Leadership, 40,* 48-49.

Chilman, C. (1981). Some angles on parent-teacher learning. *Childhood Education, 58,* 119-125.

Coit, L. (1981). Community relations, pancake style. *The American School Board Journal, 168,* 34-40.

Conant, M. (1981). Teachers and parents: Changing roles and goals. *Childhood Education, 58,* 114-118.

Criscuolo, N. (1981). Parents and the reading program. *The English Journal, 71,* 42-43.

Criscuolo, N. (1982). Parents and the secondary curriculum. *The Clearing House, 56,* 304-305.

Cross, C. (1991). The first grants: Federal leadership to advance school and family partnerships. *Phi Delta Kappan, 72*(5), 383-388.

Dauber, S. & Epstein, J. (1989). Parent attitudes and practices of parent involvement in inner-city elementary and middle schools (CREMS Report No. 32). Baltimore: Johns Hopkins University. ERIC: ED 314152.

Davies, D. (1991). Schools reaching out: Family, school, and community partnership for student success. *Phi Delta Kappan, 72*(5), 376-382.

Davis, B. (1989). A successful parent involvement program. *Educational Leadership, 47*(2), 21-23.

Dolly, J. , & Page, D. (1983). An attempt to increase parental involvement in rural schools. *Phi Delta Kappan, 64,* 512.

Epstein, J. (1987). What principals should know about parent involvement. *Principal, 66*(3), 6-9.

Epstein, J., & Becerk, H. (1982). Teachers' reported practices of parent involvement: problems and possibilities. *The Elementary School Journal, 83,* 103-113.

Epstein, J. & Dauber, S. (1989). Teacher attitudes and practices of parent involvement in inner-city elementary and middle schools (CREMS Report No. 32). Baltimore: Johns Hopkins University. ERIC: ED 314151.

Epstein, J. & Dauber, S. (1991). School programs and teacher practices of parent involvement in inner-city elementary and middle schools. *The Elementary School Journal, 91*(3), 289-305.

Esposito, L. (1982). Improving parent workshops. *The Reading Teacher, 36*(1), 90-93.

Fredericks, A. & Rasinski,T. (1990). Involving the uninvolved: How to (working with parents). *The Reading Teacher, 43*(6), 424-425.

Fredericks, A. & Rasinski, T. (1990). Working with parents: Resources for parental programs. *The Reading Teacher, 44*(3), 266-267.

Gallup, G. (1978). The tenth annual Gallup poll of the public's attitudes toward the public schools. *Phi Delta Kappan, 60,* 33-45.

Georgiady, N. & Romano, L. (1982). Parent teacher conferences. *Middle School Journal, 14*(1), 30-31.

Greenwood, G. & Hickman, C. (1991). Research and practice in parental involvement: Implications for teacher education. *The Elementary School Journal, 91*(3), 279-288.

Grossnickle, D. (1981). A checklist for teachers: Successful school and community relations. *NASSP Bulletin, 65,* 75-77.

Haley-James, S. & Nelms, V. (1980). Resources for parents of early adolescents. *Middle School Journal, 11*(3), 10-11.

Hamilton, M. (1980). Art appreciation and parent volunteers. *School Arts, 79*(9), 56-61.

Heid, C. & Harris, J. (1989). Parent involvement: A link between schools and minority communities. *Community Education Journal, 16*(4), 26-28.

Hertz, K. (1988). What part should parents play in the schools? *PTA Today, 14*(1), 6-7.

Hoerr, T. (1989). Parent surveys can give you useful information. *Educational Leadership, 47*(2), 38.

Hubert, B. (1989). Students belong in the "parent teacher" conference, too. *Educational Leadership, 47*(2), 30.

Jackson, B. & Cooper, B. (1989). Parent choice and empowerment: New roles for parents. *Urban Education, 24*(3), 263-286.

Jenkins, P. (1981). Building parent participation in urban schools. *Principal, 61*(3), 20-23

Jennings, W. (1989). How to organize successful parent advisory committees. *Educational Leadership, 47*(2), 42-45.

Johnston, H. (1990). *The New American Family and The School.* Columbus, OH: National Middle School Association.

Kahn, A. (1989). Enlisting parents' help with mathematics. *Educational Leadership, 47*(2), 37.

Lindle, J. (1989). Take parents seriously, and they'll get seriously involved. *Executive Educator, 11*(11), 24-25.

Lindle, J. (1989). What do parents want from principals and teachers. *Educational Leadership, 47*(2), 12-14.

Love, M. (1989). The home visit — an irreplaceable tool. *Educational Leadership, 47*(2), 29.

Lueder, D. (1989). Tennessee parents were invited to participate—and they did. *Educational Leadership, 47*(2), 15-17.

Manning, M. (1984). Toward an effective student, parent, middle school partnership, *Middle School Journal, 15*(4), 26-27.

McDaniel, T. (1982). Bridging the home-school gap. *NAASP Bulletin, 66*, 99-106.

Menacker, J. (1988). Parent-teacher cooperation in schools serving the urban poor. *The Clearing House, 62*(3), 108-112.

Merenda, D. (1989). Partners in education: An old tradition renamed. *Educational Leadership, 47*(2), 4-7.

Millet, W. (1980). Working with parents. *Instructor, 89*, 52-58.

Moles, O. (1982). Synthesis of research on parent participation in children's education. *Educational Leadership, 40*, 44-47.

Myers, J. (1985). *Involving Parents in Middle Level Education,* Columbus, OH: National Middle School Association

Moseman, M. (1982). Parents back to school. *Science and Children, 19*(7), 18-19.

Pesch, H. (1982). Parents and kids-communicating in the classroom. *The Science Teacher, 49,* 45.

Rasinski, T. & Fredericks, A. (1989). Dimensions of parent involvement (working with parents). *The Reading Teacher, 43*(2), 180-182.

Rosenau, F. (1981). Several agencies focus on encouraging parent involvement in public education. *Phi Delta Kappan, 63,* 85-86.

Scheer, J. & Henniger, M. (1982). Math clinic: An ideal setting for parental involvement. *Arithmetic Teacher, 30,* 48-51.

Schulz, J. (1982). A parent views parent participation. *Exceptional Education Quarterly, 3*(2), 17-24.

Seeley, D. (1982). Education through partnership. *Educational Leadership, 40,* 42-43.

Seeley, D. (1989). A new paradigm for parent involvement. *Educational Leadership, 47*(2), 46-48.

Silvestri, K. (1989). Educating parents for a larger role in school improvement. *Educational Leadership, 47*(2), 43.

Sittig, L (1982). Involving parents and children in reading for fun. *The Reading Teacher, 36*(2), 166-168.

Stahl, N. & Brown, W. (1981). Help is out there — here's how to find it. *Instructor, 91,* 80-84.

Stanic, G. (1989). Parental involvement in a time of changing demographics. *Arithmetic Teacher, 37*(4), 33-35.

Suchara, H. (1982). Parents and teachers: A partnership. *Childhood Education, 58,* 130-133.

Sullivan, E. (1980). Parent drop-in center. *Teacher, 97,* 46.

Swick, K. et al. (1980). Teachers-students-parents: They need each other. *Middle School Journal, 11*(4), 3, 24.

Torney P. (1990). "Family night" brings parents to school. *Middle School Journal, 22*(2), 34-35.

Valeri-Gold, M. (1990). Back to basics: Getting parents involved. *Reading Today, 8*(3), 14.

Van Devender, E. (1988). Involving parents: How and why. *Academic Therapy, 23*(5), 523-528.

Warner, I. (1991). Parents in touch: District leadership for parent involvement. *Phi Delta Kappan, 72*(5), 372-375.

Williams, D. & Chavkin, N. (1989). Essential elements of strong parent involvement programs. *Educational Leadership, 47*(2), 18-20.

Wolf, J. & Stephens, T. (1989). Parent/teacher conferences: Finding common ground. *Educational Leadership, 47*(2), 28-31.

Organizations

The following organizations (Williams & Chavkin, 1989) are excellent sources of information on involving family members in middle level programs and activities.

Appalachia Educational Laboratory, P.O. Box 1348, Charleston, WV 25325. (304) 347-0400

National Congress of Parents and Teachers, 1201 16th Street, NW #619, Washington, DC 20036. (202) 822-7878

Center for Early Adolescence, University of North Carolina, Chapel Hill, Suite 233, Carr Mill Mall, Carrboro, NC 27510. (919) 966-1148

National School Boards Association, 1680 Duke Street, Alexandria, VA 22314 .(703) 838-6722

Center on Parent Involvement, Johns Hopkins University, c/o Joyce Epstein, 3505 N. Charles St., Baltimore, MD. 21218 (301) 338-7570

National School Volunteer Program, 701 N. Fairfax, St. #320, Alexandria, VA 22314. (703) 836-4480

Cornell University Family Matters Project, 7 Research Park, Cornell University, Ithaca, NY 14850. (607) 255-2080 or 255-2531

Parent Involvement Center, Chapter 1 Technical Assistance Center, RMC Research Corporation, 400 Lafayette Rd. Hampton, NH 03842. (603) 926-8888

Council of the Great City School, 1413 K St., N.W., 4th Floor, Washington, DC 20005. (202) 635-5431

Parent Involvement in Education, San Diego County Office of Education, c/o Janet Chrispeels, 6401 Linda Vista Rd., Rm. 407, San Diego, CA 92111-7399. (619) 292-3500

Home and School Institute, 1201 16th Street, N.W., Washington, DC 20036. (202) 466-3633

Institute for Responsive Education, 605 Commonwealth Avenue, Boston, MA 02215. (617) 353-3902

Southwest Educational Development Laboratory, 211 E. Seventh St., Austin, TX 78701. (512) 476-6861

National Coalition for Parent Involvement in Education, 119 N. Payne Street, Alexandria, VA 22314. (703) 683-6232

University of California/State Department of Education Joint Task Force on Parent Involvement, c/o Susan Brand, Department of Education, University of California at Berkeley, Berkeley, CA 95064. (415) 526-3864

National Committee for Citizens in Education, 10840 Little Patuxent Pkwy., #301, Columbia, MD 21044-3199.(301) 977-9300 (800) 638-9675

Center for Family Resources, 384 Clinton St., Hempstead, NY 11550. (516) 489-3716

Work and Family Research Council, The Conference Board, Inc., 845 Third Ave., New York, NY 10022. (202) 759-0900

Family Resource Coalition, 230 N. Michigan Avenue, Suite 1625, Chicago, IL 60601. (312) 726-4750

National Community Education Association, 119 N. Payne Street, Alexandria, VA 22314. (703) 683-NCEA

National Association of Partners in Education 601 Wythe Street, Suite 200, Alexandria, VA 22314 (703) 836-4880

School-Age Child Care Project Center for Research on Women, Wellesley College, Wellesley, MA 02181 (617) 431-1453

Parents as Teachers National Center, Marillac Hall, University of Missouri-St. Louis, 8001 Natural Bridge, St. Louis, MO 63121. (314) 553-5738

Cooperative Communication Between Home and School, Department of Human Development and Family Studies, Cornell Cooperative Extension, G-91 MVR Hall, Cornell University, Ithaca, NY. 14853 (607) 255-2531

School Age NOTES, P.O. Box 120674, Nashville, TN 37212. (615) 292-4957

Center for Research on Elementary and Middle Schools, Dissemination Office, The Johns Hopkins University, 3505 North Charles Street Baltimore, MD 21218

References Cited

Bauch, J. (1989). The Trans*Parent* school model: New technology for parent involvement. *Educational Leadership, 47* (2), 32-34.

Carnegie Council on Adolescent Development (1989). *Turning Points: Preparing American Youth for the 21st Century.* New York: Carnegie Corporation.

Dauber, S. & Epstein, J. (1989). Parent attitudes and practices of parent involvement in inner-city elementary and middle schools (CREMS Report No. 32). Baltimore: Johns Hopkins University. ERIC: ED 314152

Davis, B. (1989) A successful parent involvement program. *Educational Leadership, 47* (2), 21-23.

Epstein, J. (1987). What principals should know about parent involvement. *Principal, 66* (3), 6-9.

Epstein, J. & Dauber, S. (1989). Teacher attitudes and practices of parent involvement in inner-city elementary and middle schools (CREMS Report No. 32). Baltimore: Johns Hopkins University. ERIC: ED 314151.

Epstein, J. & Dauber, S. (1991). School programs and teacher practices of parent involvement in inner-city elementary and middle schools. *The Elementary School Journal, 91* (3), 289-305.

Gallup, G. (1978). The tenth annual Gallup poll of the public's attitudes toward the public schools. *Phi Delta Kappan, 60,* 33-45.

Greenwood, G. & Hickman, C. (1991). Research and practice in parent involvement: Implications for teacher education. *The Elementary School Journal, 91* (3), 279-288.

Johnston, H. (1990). *The New American Family and the School.* Columbus, OH: National Middle School Association.

Lindle, J. (1989). What do parents want from principals and teachers. *Educational Leadership, 47* (2), 15-17.

Lueder, D. (1989). Tennessee parents were invited to participate — and they did. *Educational Leadership, 47* (2), 15-17.

Merenda, D. (1989). Partners in education: An old tradition renamed. *Educational Leadership, 47* (2), 4-7.

Moles, O. (1982). Synthesis of research on parent participation in children's education. *Educational Leadership, 40,* 44-47.

Myers, J. (1985). *Involving parents in middle level education.* Columbus, OH: National Middle School Association.

Williams, D. & Chavkin, N. (1989). Essential elements of strong parent involvement programs. *Educational Leadership, 47* (2), 18-20.